CHOOSE
TO BE

Free

James Holland, Sr.

Published by
The WORDPRO Press
Printed in Ithaca, New York

ISBN # 0-9753571-9-0

Choose To Be Free
by James M. Holland

Acknowledgements

I would like to thank Cynthia Joyce and my dear wife Shirline for interpreting my writing, proof reading and typing my manuscripts.

Special thanks to the many who encouraged me to present this material.

Table of Contents

Choose to be Free

CHOOSE TO BE FREE

How do we choose to be free ? Can we really be free from emotional and spiritual bondage? Can one really have the mind of Christ ? Can we be free from an unforgiving attitude? Free from bitterness, from prejudices from fear, from wrong preconceived ideas?

The answer to these questions and many more that fit into this arena of life is a resounding **YES,YES,YES.**

We must choose to make right choices based on the principles of what the Word teaches. We must learn how to get the **word working in us, not merely having a mental** understanding of it.. As James puts it we must through the act of obedience have works to accompany our faith. Our world desperately needs to know there is a real freedom that we can have. Freedom from guilt, from shame, freedom from anger, from wrong thinking, freedom from our past failures. The ability to really forgive one another. We will endeavor through the following pages to see how we can apply the life changing scriptures to our daily lives so that not only we can be victorious but that we may have a positive influence on the lives of others as well.

Freedom begins with a choice that only we can make. We must understand that it is not God's fault if we are not free, it's our choice. We must cast off this **victim mentality** that our society is so accustomed to. This mind set has even entered the circles of Christianity No doubt you have heard it said that " knowledge is power", that's only half right. Let me explain before you lay this book down.

CHOOSE TO BE FREE

Many have knowledge of what they should do, yet they do not have the aggressive will power to apply that knowledge to their current circumstances. The truth is Knowledge with action is power! !t is time for the household of faith to put into action the knowledge of the word of God that lies dormant in our hearts.

So if you are brave enough! If you are tired of being a normal Christian if you want real joy, real victory, life changing victory, head turning victory, devil scaring victory then read on my faithful friend. Apply these Biblical principles to your life and let's go change a world and help others **CHOOSE TO BE FREE.**

ROMANS 8:2
THERE IS THEREFORE NOW NO CONDEMNATION TO THEM WHICH ARE IN CHRIST JESUS, WHO WALK NOT AFTER THE FLESH, BUT AFTER THE SPIRIT.

Free From Fear

Philippians 4:6,7
"Do not be anxious about anything, but in everything by prayer and petitions, with thanksgiving, present your request to God. And the peace of God, which passes all understanding, will guard your hearts and minds through Christ Jesus."

It is quite unreasonable for us to think that all of us do not feel fear in our lives from time to time. Especially in light of all that is happening in our world today. Fear is a basic reaction to the unknown or to any kind of threat to us or those whom we love. It serves us well in the normal course of events because it keeps us from doing anything that would harm us. But, like so many other healthy functions, fear can become distorted. It is then that fear can itself become the source of harm. We must learn how to keep our fears contained and reality based. What I mean by this is that while we must allow ourselves to feel fear when there is a real threat ,yet at the same time we must challenge our thinking about fear when it isn't real.

It is in these areas of our thinking that our imaginations can work against us. If not corrected through applying the word of God to our daily battles of life. There are many scripture verses that can comfort us when we are fearful.

Share Your Fears With God

God offers us His peace for dealing with real fears. We must be careful not to pray in such a way as to make us more fearful! Many today pray in the mind set of "fear hoping" instead of " "faith believing". When you pray from the mind set of fear hoping all you are doing is incubating your fearful thoughts, your fear actually increases instead of decreasing.

You set the stage for the enemy to move in and take advantage of your situation.

Pray and ask God for three things when you are battling with fear. **(1)** A greater understanding of what is really going on in your life that is making you afraid. **(2)** For a deeper understanding of the reality of His love and protection. **(3)** For the courage and strength to step out of your unreasonable fears into the presence of God's peace.

Our fears are magnified when we shoulder our own worries, cares, and fears. Then we begin to collapse under the weight of it all. This kind of fear is not a Godly attitude because it reveals an unwillingness to trust God. **What!** How can this be? I am a born again believer you say, well I am certainly not here to challenge that, but I am telling you that many in the household of faith are not free from the fears that the spiritual world tries to put on them as well as the unfounded fears that many well meaning Christians seem to have, an over abundant supply to share with everyone. You need to read and release **1 Peter 5:7 "casting all your care on Him, for He cares for you"** into your spirit and your thinking process, this will help you develop the mind of Christ in your mind. What is the "mind of Christ?" Simply put, the ability to approach life's challenges as well as the spiritual battles we face with the same mind set that Christ would have toward them. How? By knowing and releasing the word of God into our lives. This is what will bring freedom to us over fear.

Fear

Fear is the natural and necessary alarm system that is triggered whenever we feel threatened. We must remember that this emotion ignites a response to a **real** or **perceived** danger. Many feel fear over **imagined** possible outcomes. When this fear is left unchallenged it will produce a **negative based** mind set. You will begin to imagine the worst of every situation. Our society has created a perfect climate for fear, worry, and anxiety! It is true that we live in a very violent world. Yet, as believers we can not and must not let the mind sets of an unbelieving world dictate to us how we will think and live. Listen to some encouraging statements from the word.

1 Peter 5:7
"Casting all your care upon Him"

This scripture is a good anecdote for fear. Look closer at some of the key words. For example, casting. The word to cast literally means to "THROW UPON." That is exactly what we should do. We need to know that Christ desired deeply to carry our cares. Isaiah 53:4 declares, "He has borne our griefs and carried our sorrows." Notice it's all past tense, it's not something He is working on, it's a done deal, already taken care of. "Come unto me, all you who labor and are heavy laden and I will give you rest. Take my yoke upon you and learn of me, for My yoke is easy and My burden is light." (Matthew 11:28-30).

The key here is to learn of Him. That is to learn how to react to life's fears in the proper manner, as Christ would respond to it. The scripture in Matthew 11 is teaching us to come into agreement with what Christ has said not merely with some emotional feeling we might be experiencing.

7

Another key word that Peter uses is **ALL**. He encourages us to cast "all" of our cares upon Christ, not just what we would consider the BIG ONES! For some reason that is exactly what most of us do. Choose to be free from fear, don't allow your emotions and your thinking patterns to be controlled by uncontrollable fear. That is never the will of God!

More Helpful Scriptures

Focus on Solutions, Not on Problems.
Matthew 14:22-23

Turn to God First, Not last
1 Peter 5:7

Stop Wasting Energy Thinking About What Could Happen!
Isaiah 13:7-8
II Timothy 1:7

Keep Your Thoughts on God in Order to Have Peace
Isaiah 26:3

Pray and Release
Philippians 4:4-9
DAILY!!

Fear vs. Worry
Is there a difference?

We have already established that fear is a natural emotion. What then is worry? Millions are preoccupied with a spirit of worry!

Worry is not an emotion but a mental activity that will produce fear and anxiety. I am sure you have heard the saying, "Worry is like rocking in a rocking chair, it will keep you busy, but you won't get anywhere." This is *stinking thinking.* It is an unhealthy and unreasonable exercise that attempts to solve situations beyond our control.

Instead of praying or simply letting go of things that cannot be controlled, worriers are obsessed with trying to control the problems. I have noticed that you can't <u>pray</u> and <u>worry</u> at the same time! Guess which activity Satan would rather we be involved in!

Worry destroys our faith! Worry says the only way I can have faith is to totally understand everything that is going on! Nothing could be farther from the truth.

If the only time you obey the word of God is when you have totally figured out exactly how it's all going to turn out, then you will live in more disobedience than obedience. You also will be bound by worry and fear, instead of walking by faith in God's word. In fact, the reason so many in the house hold of faith live under the spirit of worry and fear is because they are not acting in obedience to the word, so they don't really understand what is really going on in their lives.

To really say I believe the word, means I will be obedient to what the word directs me to do. Thus, I will come into agreement with God's life changing word.

People that worry will always convince themselves and anyone else who will listen how terrible it is. They will imagine all sorts of horrible results. Worry distorts faith that is at work in our lives.

People that worry long enough will actually begin to believe that if they worry enough, then worry will somehow solve all of their problems. Don't be a charter member of the miserable majority, be an overcomer, after all, that's what Christ declared we were to be.

1 Timothy 1:7
"For God has not given us a spirit of fear, but of power and of love and a sound mind."

Anxiety

What is anxiety or anxiety disorders? We hear a lot about this condition today. In fact, I am told that anxiety disorders are the most common emotional struggles of today, affecting some 20 - 30 million people. Everyone experiences some anxiety from time to time. So, how does one know if they are battling with anxiety disorder?

Anxiety disorder can be a sudden and unexplained uneasiness that lasts a few hours, or it can be a constant state.

Psalms 91:1-2
"He who dwells in the secret place of the Most High, shall abide under the shadow of the Almighty. (2) I will say of the Lord, "He is my refuge, My God in Him I will trust."

CHOOSE TO BE FREE

To be free from anxiety we need to learn how to live the above scripture. If you are battling with fear or worry or anxiety, don't feel condemned by God. Choose to obey the word and be set free by the power of God's spirit.

Closer Look

Many Christians think that God condemns all anxiety and that by implication He also condemns those that suffer with it. Nothing could be further from the truth. Christ came to make us free.

Jesus said, "Let not your heart be troubled." (John 14:1) Notice the choice we have. "**Let not**", it implies that we can choose whether or not we will let worry, anxiety and fear control our lives instead of us controlling these things.

In the sermon on the Mount, Jesus calls attention to the destructiveness of anxiety, fear, and worry about the future.

Matthew 6:25-34

His teaching is very clear, that such fear and worry is futile, pointless and unable to help solve anything. No worrisome thought about tomorrow can help people live better lives or keep evil away.

CHOOSE TO BE FREE

Worry, then is not an emotion but a **"Thinking pattern"** that takes hold when people try to live independent of God.

Unless **fear, worry,** and **anxiety** are honestly faced and worked through by applying the knowledge of God's word to our lives and to our situations, we will live defeated unhappy lives! This is not the will of God <u>ever!</u>

Scriptures to release into our lives to defeat fear, worry, and anxiety:
Isaiah 13:7-8
Psalms 55:5
Psalms 91:5
Matthew 8:26
I John 4:1-8
Revelations 21:8

(**Pray this prayer**): In the name of Jesus, I release the love of God into my spirit, the power of the Holy Spirit to work within me and to have a sound mind each day.
In the scripture II Timothy 1:7, where it mentions "sound mind", it literally means to have a **"teachable spirit"**. That is, to receive the promises of God's word, not just mentally, but into our spirit as well, so that we can act upon the word instead of our fears or emotions.

Notice the steps given in the passage. He first points out what God has not given us! Why would we want something in our lives working that God didn't give us?

Then Paul points out how God will give us victory. First of all, He gives us **power**. Why do we need the power of the spirit? So we can have fellowship with God and so we can rightly divide the word of truth into our spirits and minds.

The power of the spirit gives us freedom. It gives us wisdom to discern everything that comes into our lives whether it's good for us or not. We need to walk in the power of the spirit not just talk about it.

The next thing God has made available is love. Why do we need the love of God in our lives? The love of God reveals to us how much God cares about us. It also drives out all the bitterness, hatred and all the other things we have allowed to come into our lives. If we don't allow God's love to flow through us, we will never receive God's forgiveness nor will we be willing to forgive others.

My friend, if we are not filled with the spirit of truth, which releases the power of the spirit into our lives, then we certainly will not receive the love of God so that we can love God and love others as well. Only when this is released in us will we have a **sound mind**, which means a teachable mind.

Remember, the choice to be free from worry and fear isn't up to your next door neighbor nor is it up to the Devil, your adversary, I might add, it isn't up to God. It's your choice. God is waiting for your decision.

CHOOSE TO BE FREE

People's attitudes reflect their perspective on life. Attitudes are formed in the mind. Every attitude begins with a choice to look at the world in a certain way. People can change their attitudes!

Romans 12:2
"And do not be conformed to this world, but be transformed by the renewing of your mind, that you prove what is that good and acceptable and perfect will of God."

One of the main causes of emotional and spiritual problems in life is "faulty thinking, such as untruthful thinking and unrealistic thinking which leads to irrational actions.

For us to live the abundant life that Christ offers, we must believe the **truth** and **live** it out in our lives. The Bible talks a great deal about our thinking. The above scripture exhorts us to renew our minds. Philippians 4:8 offers us some very powerful guidelines for correct patterns of thought. You need to read and put into practice these principles every day.

Isaiah 26:3
"Thou wilt keep him in perfect peace, whose <u>mind</u> is stayed on thee: because he trusteth in thee."

What we think plays a critical role in determining our emotional and spiritual health. God, who is truth, wants us to think and believe truth because doing so sets us free!

Satan the deceiver and "father of lies" wants us to believe his lies because they destroy us and put us in emotional and spiritual bondage. Satan has many lies in his arsenal. Here are just a couple of examples:

14

(1) "I must be perfect." Believing this lie results in believing that we can not be wrong about anything. It also makes us very judgmental! People that have these kinds of thinking problems will not pray nor will they have an ongoing diet of the word of God. Normally, they have a couple of favorite scriptures that they can always quote. This seems to justify them!

(2) "I must have everyone's love and approval." This lie leads us to focus on pleasing people more than pleasing God. So, we become performance based instead of faith based. This also causes the person to become self-centered! This was Achan's problem (Joshua 7:20-21). The rules apply to everyone except them. Achan's problem was "it had to be his way". It was all about him and what he wanted. He had no concept of how his action would effect everyone else. We can not afford to make the love and approval of others more important to us than the love and approval of God.

(3) "Things have to be my way for me to be happy". This is an unbiblical belief. It causes us to focus our attention on circumstances rather than on God.

How, then do I combat these thoughts and millions more just like these. I'm glad you asked!

It must first be understood that people can not properly renew their minds apart from God and His word. We are not merely talking about a positive thinking class. We are talking about putting the word of God into action in our lives.

We must know and obey the truth. How can we start the process of renewing our minds? First, we must start recognizing the lies that we tell ourselves. That's right! We have the tendency to deceive ourselves. Second, we must allow the word of God to scrutinize every thought that comes through our minds. And last, we must put the word in our thinking process every day.

Knowing, **believing**, and **applying** biblical truth are the three keys toward having a renewed mind and experiencing the transforming power of a relationship with God.

God is more than willing to help us believe the truth. It's a life long process, but it's one that leads to freedom. Proverbs 3:5-6, "Trust in the Lord with all your heart, and lean not on your own understanding. In all your ways acknowledge Him and He shall direct your paths."

Before you get the morning news each morning, get God's "Good News" and release it in your mind daily.

Tips for a Good Attitude

Too many Christians live lives of quiet desperation, always worrying and fretting. They pray, but peace never seems to come to their hearts. Why? They may in many cases have negative attitudes about everything. **You can't really pray** and **worry too**! You have to choose what you are going to do.

In Micah 6:8, the prophet provides three requirements which when acted upon will have an enormous impact on our attitude. Here they are:

CHOOSE TO BE FREE

1) To have a good attitude, we must "do justly". That is, we must be honest with ourselves, then we must live honestly. We must quit making excuses for our wrong actions and our wrong thinking and then start dealing with our own hearts and minds. We must be willing to admit and face our own problems. After all, problems begin on the inside.

(2) The second thing, the prophet said we must do is to "love mercy". What is he saying to us? Here it is, we must learn to make things right. If it is a problem between people then someone has to take the step to make it right.

(3) We must "walk humbly" with God. We need to ask God to search our minds and hearts daily.

Just as a bad attitude can become a way of life, so can a good attitude. So, God is not asking us to do something that is impossible.

Christians who spend time daily in God's word and in prayer, who cast their cares upon Him and who seek to obey God's word in all circumstances will have the presence of God, the peace of God, and the power of God in their lives.

Release these scriptures into your life:

Philippians 2:5-11
Philippians 4:13
Acts 27:22
II Corinthians 10:5
Galatians 6:9
James 1:2-4

CHOOSE TO BE FREE

Pray this prayer. "In the Name of Jesus, I pray for and release the mind of Christ into my life. I will not be conformed by the thinking of the world, but by the word of God".

BE FREE!!

Free From Depression

CHOOSE TO BE FREE

At times, everyone feels sad, down, and what we would call feeling blue. Solomon wrote of "a time to weep" and "a time to mourn" (Ecclesiastes 3:4). Also the writer of Hebrews assured us that we would have time of need in our lives (Hebrews 4:16).

If we are going to be free from depression, we must first understand what it is. Depression is a deep level of emotional turmoil and it effects many people in and out of the church in many different ways. It can also be magnified by a spiritual attack from our enemy, Satan! This is not to say that everyone who deals with depression is demonized as some have wrongly declared!

Psalms 130:1-2
Out of the depths I have cried to you O Lord: Lord hear my voice!
Let your ears be attentive to the voice of my supplications.

According to recent research, one person in five will experience significant and persistent levels of depression that will cause them to miss more work than diabetes and heart disease!

Depression affects individuals families, coworkers and all others who are in regular contact with the depressed person.

What causes depression?

Depression can be caused by a variety of things, including stress, fear, loneliness, guilt, and anger. David wrote about his depression that was brought on by unconfessed sin (Psalms 38).

Depression can also be brought on by a number of medical factors as well. This is why anyone who is experiencing extended bouts of depression should have a medical checkup If there is not a problem there, then we must turn our attention to correcting the problem from a spiritual approach.

There were many in the Bible who struggled with depression. Moses, the great leader of Israel, had times of depression. (Exodus 17:4) "What shall I do unto this people? They be almost ready to stone me."

Job battled with depression, "my soul is weary of my life" (Job 10:1).
Elijah was depressed after a great victory. He actually wanted to die! (I Kings 19:4). Many other Bible characters shared the lonely path of depression.
Does this mean that we should just expect to be depressed and just try somehow to deal with it? NO! NO! NO! God wants us to have victory in our lives. Yet, because we are human, we will feel these emotions and have to deal with them. That is the key, to knowing how to deal with it.
So we can walk in the victory that God wants us to enjoy.

CHOOSE TO BE FREE

Symptoms of Depression

In Psalms 102, King David provides a check list of symptoms. Let's look at some of them:

(1) "Let my cry come to you. Do not hide your face from me in the day of my trouble" (Psalms 102:1-2). He continues to write of how he feels stricken physically and described losing meaning and purpose in His life. "My days are consumed like smoke, and my bones are burned like a hearth. My heart is stricken and withered like grass" (verse 3-4). He lost his appetite (verse 4), "I forget to eat my bread."

He felt isolated and rejected and all alone. "I am like a pelican of the wilderness; I am like an owl of the desert" (verse 6). He couldn't sleep (verse 7), "I lie awake." He had crying spells. "I have eaten ashes like bread and magnified my drink with weeping" (verse 9). This is a pretty despairing picture isn't it? Yet millions are living in this situation currently. Let me say at this point that many Christians are depressed, because in many cases the church has not been instructed biblically on how to respond to these needs. They are afraid to step out and come for help!

Respond to Depression

As I mentioned earlier, Elijah the Great Prophet also had bouts of depression. He demonstrated both healthy and unhealthy ways to respond to depression.

CHOOSE TO BE FREE

Closer Look

The story is in (I Kings 19). After the great victory on Mount Carmel, his life was threatened by Queen Jezebel and he became afraid! Now come on, if in fact Jezebel was going to kill the prophet, would she have really sent him a telegram declaring it? It would have been much easier just to ambush him and take him prisoner than kill him! The truth is she did not have the authority to do this because God's hand was on Elijah! What was the determining factor then that caused Elijah the man of faith to respond this way?

The scripture says Elijah was afraid! So then, fear brought on his depression. One of Satan's greatest weapons yet today, is the spirit of fear that he tries to release on people especially God's people. This is why we must understand spiritual authority! We will discuss spiritual authority later. Now back to the story. Elijah became depressed because he was afraid, because he focused on the situation at hand instead of on the power of God!

Psalms 27:1

"The Lord is my light and my salvation, in whom shall I fear? The Lord is the strength of my life, of whom shall I be afraid?"

CHOOSE TO BE FREE

During a sequence of events, Elijah sank deeper and deeper into a depressed state. His fear became so intense that he ran away, isolated himself, and prayed that he would die (verse 4). At his most depressed state he was:

Hungry - He stopped eating.

Angry He was mad at God.

Lonely - He left his servant and traveled alone!

Tired - He collapsed into sleep!

Now, notice every forward motion in his life came to a **HALT.** This is always the result of depression.

Now the Good News

God counteracted this HALT in his life at every level. God provided food for Elijah. He sent an angel. The angel reminded Elijah that he was not alone. Two times God encouraged Elijah to regain his strength by eating, drinking, and resting. God brought him out which enabled Elijah to focus on God and not on his fear (verse 15:18). The story reminds us of the importance of having a real relationship with God. If you are depressed, know that you can be free.

CHOOSE TO BE FREE

Resist the urge to run from the situation and avoid isolation, especially from the body of Christ. God is ready to help us overcome this time of difficulty in our lives! We must receive God's help in this area.

Release these Promises in Your Life

Psalms 34:1-8	Psalms 88:1-18
Psalms 40:1-3	Psalms 143:1
Psalms 42:1-11	Psalms 147:3
Psalms 43:1-5	Isaiah 41:10
Romans 8:18-39	II Corinthians 1:8-11

The Other Side of Despair

The word hopeless has no place in the believers vocabulary. If the Lord is present so is hope in every situation! God's word offers hope regardless of how dark and desperate a situation may seem (I Corinthians 13:13).

Anchor your hope in Christ (I Peter 3:15,16) Nothing can separate us from the love of God except we allow it to do so (Romans 8:38). Any problem or affliction we face will pale in comparison with the power of God that He desires to release in us!

We must learn to look beyond our immediate circumstances, beyond the worry, and the despair that so easily grips us. Look to the Light of God's work that gives hope and deliverance when properly applied to out lives!

The believer is never without hope, no matter how we may feel! We are never beyond the reach of God's hand of grace and mercy. Even when we are struggling. If you are battling with despair push on through that valley. Do it quickly!! Don't allow despair to rob you of God's blessings for your life.

The Importance of Hope

We must have hope or life isn't worth the living! At least that's the way we feel! Satan loves it when we operate in despair and fear rather than in hope! Despair paralyzes our faith and our actions. It also becomes contagious. We can pass despair on to our family just as we can pass hope on to them.

God will bring people into our lives and I call them "divine appointments" that will help us get through those times of despair. Israel was in despair at the banks of the Jordan after the twelve spies had returned. Let's follow their steps to see what happened! The story unfolds in Deuteronomy 1: notice **verse 25.** "And they took the fruit of the land in their hands, and bought it down to us, and bought us word again, and said it is a good land which the Lord our God doth give **us**". Sounds great, yet in verse 26 they would "**not go up**" and it gets worse in verse 27. We see the results of despair, "**and ye murmured in your tents.** "Then in verse 28: they ask how shall we go up? **"Our brethen have discouraged our hearts, saying the people are greater than we."**

Despair distorts your focus and vision and you simply can not see clearly. Eyes that <u>look</u> are <u>common</u>, eyes that <u>see</u> are <u>rare</u>! Notice they testified that the land was as God had said, yet their despair kicked in! We need to testify of the goodness of God in church but what about verse 27 - "they murmured in their tents!" What are we saying at home to our family? Are we planting seeds of despair or seeds of hope!

If their is no hope in the church their certainly can't be any in the world. Too many believe their feelings of despair and doubt their faith. All of what we are, good or bad is what we have thought and believed. What we have become is due to the price we paid to get what we wanted! Israel defeated themselves. So do we many times.

We see things not as they are, **(but as we are)!** By the way we position ourselves we will see God everywhere or no where. When we are under the influence of despair we see Him no where. Satan loves this. Don't let despair blind you to the blessing of God in your life. Notice the difference between **NO WHERE** and **NOW HERE** is where you place the emphasis.

Who discouraged these Israelites? Verse 28 gives the answer, "our brethen." If we depend totally on human ability to deal with life we will no doubt live in despair! But if we believe the promise of God then we will not only live in hope, we spread that hope to others where ever we may be. When hope arises in our spirit then we focus on verse 30, look at it: **"The Lord your God which goeth before you, He shall fight for you, according to all that He did for you in Egypt <u>before</u> <u>your</u> <u>eyes</u>."**

God was ready to lead them on and deliver what He had promised. So is He ready to do this for us! We see here what stopped the Israelites, but what is it that is stopping us? If you are in despair God's word to you is <u>go</u> <u>forward</u>, don't stay there! Rise up, reach up, get hold of some hope, and go forward! Israel chose to be defeated because despair had set in on them. We too must make a choice each and every day. Let's choose to live in Hope instead of despair!

Scriptures to help release Hope

John 16:33	Psalms 42:5
Romans 5:3-5	Hebrews 13:5
Isaiah 58:11	I John 4:4

Free From Unforgiveness

Millions in the body of Christ as well as outside of the body are bound by the emotional chains of unforgiveness. I am convinced that the partial cause of this is many have a lack of understanding about what forgiveness is and how to properly apply it in our lives. Neither do they understand the tremendous spiritual, emotional, and physical impact unforgiveness has on the individual that is battling with it!

Unforgiveness has no Foresight

Unforgiveness is the one guaranteed formula for smothering our vision. When you have been wronged, a poor memory is your best response! **Never carry a grudge, the load is far too heavy!**

Forgive your enemies, nothing annoys them more. There is no revenge so sweet as forgiveness. **"The only people you should try to get even with are those who have helped you."** It was Henry Ward Beecher who said, "Forgiveness ought to be like a canceled note, TORN IN TWO AND BURNED UP," so that it never can be shown against one." Never is God operating in your life so strong as when you fore go revenge and dare to forgive an injury. The real question on the floor about handling revenge is this. "Are we going to let God handle it", or "will we handle it?" He who cannot forgive destroys the bridge over which he may one day need to pass. Hate, bitterness, and revenge are luxuries none of us can really afford. It's amazing that people need loving most when they deserve it the least. Forgiveness heals, unforgiveness wounds.

Matthew 5:25 (L.B.) declares, "come to terms quickly with your enemy before it is too late." The best healing is a quick healing.

No one ever gets ahead while they are trying to get even! Being offended is a strategy of Satan's to get you out of the will of God. When we focus on our offenses, trouble grows. When we focus on God, trouble goes.. When you don't forgive, you are ignoring it's impact on your life. Hate is a prolonged form of the suicide of your dreams.

Forgive your enemies, you can't get back at them any other way. Forgiveness saves the expense of anger, the high cost of hatred and the waste of energy. There are two marks of a Christian giving and forgiving. If you want to be miserable, hate somebody. Unforgiveness does a great deal more damage to the vessel in which it is stored than the object in which it is poured! So learn to forgive so you can keep your vision clear.

Prison of the Past

Unforgiveness builds prison walls around us. Life has many challenges, in fact, life is a series of challenges. So we must learn how to lighten our load.

By lightening our load I mean knowing when to release things. One of the most dangerous things is to be shackled to your past. Unforgiveness guarantees this. We all make mistakes, we all have regrets but we must learn how to live beyond them. Not in them. Life is too short to allow yourself to be an inmate in the prison of bad choices and weak decisions.

The prison of unforgiveness comes with jailers of guilt and rejection. Together they will hold you captive, torturing you with images of what could have been.

What's so unfortunate about this is that most of us don't realize that the KEY to release ourselves is within our own hands. We
need to remember that there is only ONE righteous judge and He is
forgiving! Isaiah 55:7 declares, "let the wicked forsake his way, and
the unrighteous man his thoughts, let him return unto the Lord, and
He will have mercy on him for He will abundantly pardon." To not
forgive is a sign of unrighteousness at work in us. We don't need to
spend our lives in the grave yard of unforgiveness dealing with the
corpses of our past. Know when things are dead, know when to release them, and know when to bury them. If you continue to work
with the dry bones of dead issues you too will begin to decay. Sign
the death certificate and bury the past through forgiving. Focus
your energy on the things you can actually make an impact on. I
have spent countless hours of time counseling people who have lost
precious moments of their lives because they were busy struggling
with issues that should have been already put to rest. How much
more productive and how much more fulfilling their lives could
have been if they would have just faced lingering issues and put
them to rest. Forgiveness is the key that unlocks the door to the
prison of the past.

Scriptures to Apply
Matthew 6:12   Mark 11:255
Luke 6:37   I John 1:9

CHOOSE TO BE FREE

Give Someone Your
Yesterday's Today

Sometimes we go through things not so much for us but for the sake of someone else. Your yesterdays may be someone else's today. God may be preparing you to free their today out of your yesterday experiences. That doesn't mean that you won't wonder why such things are happening to you at this time.

Hindsight is an invaluable way to learn how things fit into God's plan. There is no such thing as "waste" in God's economy. He knows exactly what He is doing.

God led Moses, the prince of Egypt, and murderer into the "desert of relinquishment" to teach him to be a shepherd and deliverer. It was there Moses learned many of the things he needed to lead Israel through the Sinai. David was also familiar with the process of relinquishment. He was the one who wrote "yea though I walk through the valley of the shadow of death" (Psalms 23:4). All of us will experience our own valleys and feel the cold shadow of death on our shoulders at times. This is why when everything is cold around us our spirit must be warm toward God so that we will be willing to forgive. David the same man who lived in a cave as an exile and outlaw and later ran for his life when his own son plotted to kill him has some words of wisdom for us. The psalmist who endured decades of relinquishment while again running from Saul's army said, "If you are in the valley of the shadow, just keep walking."

What you need is an uninterrupted walk with God, even if He takes you throughout the dark valley. Just don't wallow in it! Don't linger there, don't pitch your tent under that shadow. Above all, don't throw a "pity party" in that valley. Just forgive, forgive, forgive.

36

Because until we forgive, God cannot and will not lead us out of the valley! If we want to help our family, our friends, and others be free, then we must first be free ourselves. We can't give away what we don't possess.

Your trial today can give strength to someone else later.

Forgiveness
"What is it?

Matthew 18:21-35: In verse 21 of Chapter 18 of Matthew's writing, the question is asked by Peter. "Lord how often shall my brother sin against me, and I forgive him?"

We must realize that if we are going to live free of unforgiveness, then we can't have a "calculator mind." What is forgiveness? The Greek word for forgiveness means "remission or a setting free from guilt or debt."

As we discuss how to apply forgiveness to our lives let's reveal some myths that people have concerning forgiveness!

1. Some people think that if they are not at fault they have no need to seek forgiveness. Biblical forgiveness however is not about who is at fault but rather do I want to be free or bound by the circumstance. I choose to be free!

2. Others think that if they forgive someone, yet the individual doesn't receive it, or doesn't respond by forgiving as well, that their forgiveness is not effective. Nothing could be farther from the truth. When we forgive someone regardless of how they respond, we have just set ourselves free to move forward. We are no longer bound by that circumstance. It is up to the other party or parties involved to decide if they too want to be free. It's their CHOICE.

CHOOSE TO BE FREE

The Bible teaches us that forgiveness is a Christian duty. We are commanded to forgive. "Be ye kind one to another, tenderhearted, forgiving one another, even as God for Christ's sake hath forgiven you" (Ephesians 4:32). We have needed, do need, and will need forgiveness, not only from God, but from others as well. Ultimately our own forgiveness depends upon our willingness to forgive others. "For if we forgive men their transgresses, your heavenly Father will also forgive you: but if we forgive not men their trespasses, neither will your Father forgive your trespasses" (Matthew 6:14,15).

When I forgive I am establishing the spiritual seat of authority in my life which should always be the word of God. When I refuse to forgive I am submitting my seat of authority to the one whom I refuse to forgive. Why will God not forgive me? Because I have made a choice to harbor unforgiveness and wrong feelings. I choose this and God will always honor our choice even when it is wrong. God will only work and release into our lives at what ever level we choose to allow him to work. Think about it, that person you detest or that circumstance you can't let go of has become the binding control factor in your life and it will remain that way until you choose to do something about it. You can't pray enough, sing enough, worship enough, cry enough, or complain enough to change it. You can choose to forgive and you will be set free!

Failure to forgive destroys your peace of mind. You feel knotted up inside and dirty when you know that all is not well between yourself and others. Failure to forgive destroys your usefulness and productivity. You spend all your time plotting and scheming looking for opportunities to gain revenge.

CHOOSE TO BE FREE

Failure to forgive can destroy your physical life. Ahithophel, the grandfather of Bethsheba, would not forgive David for seducing his grand daughter. He dedicated his life to getting even. His plot backfired, and he ended up taking his own life by hanging himself (II Samuel 17:23).

Failure to forgive can destroy your soul. When you face eternity in need of forgiveness, you may find that because you locked out forgiveness from your heart, you too will then be locked out from God. When you don't forgive, instead of joy our soul has misery, instead of being free we are in bondage, we can't love, we can only hate, find fault and complain, that's what unforgiveness does to people.

Choose to Forgive

"Even as Christ forgave you, so also do ye
(Colossians 3:13)

True forgiveness is unsolicited, by that I mean it shouldn't have to be asked for. Romans 5:8 declares that "While we were yet sinners, Christ died for us." Before we even ask for forgiveness God had already provided it. Don't wait until someone asks you to forgive them, if you know it needs to be done, do it!!

True forgiveness is complete. When we truly forgive we don't attach any requirements. Neither do we remind them every few days that we have forgiven them. It's done, let it go, by doing so you are setting yourself free.

True forgiveness is continuous. Forgiveness is not a one time act. It is a process, a lifestyle, if we want to live free!

39

Christ has forgiven us, He does forgive us, and He will continue to forgive us.

"Whosoever confesseth and foresaketh (his sins) shall have mercy" (Proverbs 28:13).   Unforgiveness is a sin.

Apply these scriptures

Jeremiah 31:34	Jeremiah 33:8
Micah 7:18,19	Romans 12:19

Remember, if we don't forgive then we will be bound. In fact the very things that we have been delivered from will come back to torment us. So make that choice. Do it right now. Take a few minutes, lay this book down and pray this prayer.

"In the Name of Jesus, I release the power of the Holy Spirit within me to help me forgive who ever or what ever I need to. I choose to be free from the bondage of unforgiveness. I claim my deliverance right now in Jesus Name."

Now go make it right my friend. If there are others that you need to forgive, do it. Then add them to your prayer list and call their name before the throne of God. The fact that you can pray for them is evidence that you have forgiven.

We don't go around or speak to people we haven't forgiven! So is your prayer list growing or dying?

Free From Bitterness

(Ephesians 4:13)

CHOOSE TO BE FREE

Ephesians 4:31 states, "let all bitterness and wrath, and anger, and clamor and evil speaking be put away from you with all malice."

Bitterness is the product of unforgiveness. Unfortunately, there are many people that live very bitter lives. Hardships press us up against God. How we respond makes all the difference in the world. Life has a way of challenging us even when we don't want to be challenged. I have noticed that on a lake where there are two or more sail boats, the wind that is blowing across the lake, the same wind, not several different winds, but the same wind will take each boat in the direction they desire to go. How does this happen? It's all in the adjusting of the sails. Bitterness, my friend will rip the sails off of your boat of life. It has been said that life and circumstances will either make us better or bitter! The choice is ours.

Overcoming bitterness is a difficult thing to do on our own. That's why many resolve to just live bitter lives of defeat instead of choosing to be healed. One of the things that makes it difficult to make a new start and overcome bitterness is the sense of defeat and anger that always accompanies bitterness and a bitter spirit!

If you are going to be free from bitterness you can't just treat the symptom, you have to get to the cause of the bitterness. What has made you bitter or who has made you bitter?

Like a vicious malignancy, bitterness lodges in a persons heart. It infects his whole being with poison that can often be felt physically. It drains your strength and motivation. It undermines your plans. It robs one of efficiency. In fact, many times if gone unchecked, it shames the person into quitting and giving up with no desire to try to start over again.

There is a cure for this creeping cancer of bitterness. The great physician has it and we can get it. Divine surgery in the soul is required. The infection must be purged and destroyed.

Forgiveness cleanses us of bitterness! The Bible abounds in God's promises which guarantee to every man who wishes to avail himself of them. Deliverance from bitterness and every other sin that doth so easily come to us. However, God will not force it on us! We must make a choice, ask for it, receive it, and live free!

Dysfunction is No Excuse

Even if you have come from, or presently in a dysfunctional situation you can still be free from bitterness! We hear the term dysfunctional used a lot in our society, even in the Christian realm. Too many Christians and non-Christians today use it for an excuse for inconsistency in their lives. What is the Biblical perspective on this matter?

Genesis 4:8, "Cain talked with his brother....when they were in the field Cain rose up against Abel his brother, and slew him." In the book of Genesis we find the first fight in the first family between the first two brothers. We also find our first example of dysfunction. Cain was not only jealous of his brother but he became bitter toward him also.

We hear people giving justification for their abnormal and most often sinful behavior. The words sound good. The excuse, however, is lame. The reason the words sound good to us is because we all have a degree of dysfunction in our lives. Why? We are all descendants of Adam and Eve, our great ancestors who fell from a state of perfect function.

However, if any one person is able to rise above dysfunction, then everyone can. The power of the Gospel helps us do this.

CHOOSE TO BE FREE

I John 1:9
"If we confess our sins, He is faithful and just to forgive us."

Adam and Eve gave birth to a dysfunctional son, Cain. Murder and mayhem broke out among the first two brothers. That same spirit exists in the world today. We seem to be perfectly oblivious to the fact that we all are dealing with this.

Bitterness will assassinate your dreams, destroy your hopes, and make you a mere shell of what your potential really is. Outside of the power of the spirit of God at work in us we all will fall prey to the same jealously, anger, and bitterness that Cain manifested.

We must face the reality everyday that some of our problems stem from the fact that there is a flawed nature within us that can only be changed by the power of God. Your attitude today is something that is totally under your control. You choose! Don't blame your bitterness on your family or anyone else. Base your actions on the attitude born out of faith. Rise up right now and choose to come against the attitude that has built the prison of bitterness around you.

Free yourself from Bitterness (Hebrews 12:15)

Evidence of a spirit of bitterness are:
A. Sarcastic and critical talk
B. An inability to trust people
C. Self-pity
D. A sad countenance

CHOOSE TO BE FREE

Scriptures to release in your Life
Nehemiah 9:20   Luke 4:18
Proverbs 14:10   James 4:8

Pray this prayer! "In the Name of Jesus I take authority over the spirit of bitterness that rules my life. I break the hold it has on me and I repent of it. I release the power of the Holy Spirit into me to drive out all that is not of God. I choose to be free to walk in the power of Gods spirit. I declare it in Jesus name even now!"

Free from Offenses

Luke 17:1: "It is impossible that no offenses should come."

Many are unable to function properly in their God given calling because of the wounds and hurts that offenses have caused in their lives. They are handicapped and hindered from their full potential. An offense will imprison you and cause you to sever relationships.

It's amazing, but most often it's a fellow believer who has hurt us. So we feel not only offended but betrayed as well. II Timothy 3:2 says, "men will be lovers of themselves." We expect this from unbelievers but I remind you that Paul's letter is addressed to the CHURCH! He was talking about those within. Since Jesus made it very clear that it would be impossible to live in this world and not have the possibility of being offended we better understand how to get free from this.

46

CHOOSE TO BE FREE

In Luke 17:1, the Greek word for "offend" comes from the word skandaloh. This word refers to the part of a trap in which the bait is attached. So the word implies laying a trap in someone's way. In the Bible it is referred to as entrapment used by the enemy. OFFENSE is a tool of the devil.

ARE YOU OFFENDED?

Offended people can always be divided into two categories. The first being "those who have been treated unjustly." And the second, being "those who believe they have been treated unjustly." The results are the same; both parties submit to emotional bondage.

When a person is offended their understanding is darkened! They can't see the matter clearly. One major way Satan uses to keep a person in an offended state is to keep the offense hidden, cloaked with human pride! Pride will always keep us from admitting our true condition. Pride will keep you from dealing with truth. It distorts your vision. Pride causes a person to always view themselves as VICTIM. Those with a victim mentality will say things like, "I was mistreated and misjudged." When people believe they are innocent and falsely accused they hold back forgiveness. When we blame others and defend our own position, we are blind. We struggle to remove the **SPECK** out of our brother's eye while we have a **LOG** lodged in ours.

THE CURE!

We must again choose to except the truth about ourselves, our circumstances, and then turn to God's word for release. Unfortunately many today do not see the **TRUE CONDITIONS** of their hearts.

CHOOSE TO BE FREE

In fact, we do not see things as they are, we see them as we are!

Hebrews 3:13 states that hearts are hardened through the deceitfulness of sin! If we do not deal with an offense, it will produce more fruit of sin.

Jesus said our ability to see correctly is a key to being free. When we are offended we see ourselves as victims and blame those who hurt us. So we justify our unforgiveness, envy, and resentment. Jesus says in Revelations 3:18, "Anoint your eyes with eye salve, that you may see." See what? Our true condition! It is the revelation of truth that brings freedom to us. When the Spirit of God shows us our sin, He always does it in a way that gives us the strength to repent and be free!

APPLY THESE SCRIPTURES TO BE FREE!

REVELATION 12:11	II TIMOTHY 1:7
EPHESIANS 5:2	I JOHN 4:6
PSALMS 51:10	I PETER 1:6-7

Free From Wrong Choices

Have you ever felt it and yet didn't know how to explain it? Because life is a journey sometimes we get off the path. It's when you are off your path you can begin to feel your **soul ache**.

It's not like a toothache or a stomach ache. You feel this pain in the deepest part of your soul. There is no medication that will correct it.. The only thing that will ease an aching soul is repentance. Repentance means to turn around and go the right way, the word repentance actually implies a continual turning toward what is right.

Like all pain that comes to the human body, a soul ache is a warning that something is wrong. The pain is an alarm that sounds off when you have stepped out of your path of life that God has ordered. Your soul begins to ache to remind you that you are on the wrong road to get to the right destination. You have made a wrong choice. Psalms 42:11 asks, "why art thou cast down O my soul? And why art thou troubled within me?"

We feel these emotions when we are off track Our soul acts like a compass that helps us keep going in the right direction. Have you made some wrong choices? Welcome to the human race. The important question is not have you made wrong choices, but rather what are you doing to correct the problem. This is where the every day battle is waged! Why do we make wrong choices? There are a lot of reasons: bad information, responding out of anger, or out of some emotional feeling. The main reason we make wrong choices is because of our human spirit. **It gets in the way**! I have come to realize that most everyday people, especially those in the kingdom of God credit many of their problems and battles to Satan and his demons, make no mistake about it, Satan is real and there is a real spirit world around us. Yet, most people are not battling with demons at all.

CHOOSE TO BE FREE

They are simply battling with their **human will** that they have never brought under submission to God's word. So they are locked in prisons of their own making by the wrong choices they have made and continue to make. It's time to have a **break out**! You must choose to recover from wrong choices. In the Book of Joshua 1:8, the scriptures says, "This Book of the Law shall not depart from your mouth, but you shall meditate in it day and night, that you may observe to do according to **ALL** that is written in it. For then you will make your way prosperous, and then you will have good success." This is the only place in scripture that we find the word success. What is God saying to Joshua? He is literally telling him if you walk in agreement with my word and apply it's principals to your life, you will be victorious. Why? Because the word applied will help us make right choices. You see we must first commit to the fact that God's word is supreme. The Bible is not just a good book, there are millions of good books. The Bible is God in ink, it is His mind put on paper for us to read! The good news is we can recover from wrong choices. How do people get into the cycle of wrong choices. Let's discuss it!

CONTRIBUTORS TO WRONG CHOICES

How we view life and ourselves has a tremendous impact on what kind of choices we make. Remember, everyone in this world has been abused by sin before we came to God. We must know sin is destructive, it kills, it doesn't just make one feel bad or look bad, it kills and we need to always remember this.

Many people refuse to admit that they have made some wrong choices or even if they do admit it, they seem to want to insist that sin had nothing to do with it. Denial is a contributor to making wrong choices.

52

CHOOSE TO BE FREE

PROVERBS 29:23
"A MAN'S PRIDE SHALL BRING HIM LOW."

Our **fleshly pride** is a real enemy to us admitting wrong. People that live in denial of what is really going on with them do not need the Devil or anyone else to fight them. They will self-destruct and their world will crumble around them.

Procrastination is another contributor to making wrong choices. We may blame it on our busy schedules or prior commitments, the family or the job. The truth however is when people have been living out the nightmares of wrong choices they become afraid to commit to anything. A commitment means I have to make a choice to choose. Many go underground spiritually when they have made wrong choices and are not willing to admit it and do what is necessary to correct the action. They become lonely, guilt ridden and fearful so they turn to everything except God. This is when they enter the **EXCUSE MILL**. They start saying things like it's not really my fault, if my circumstances were different than what they are, if I had a different job, a different family, or a different church, and on and on it goes. But they never address the real problem so they continue to make bad choices. They simply recycle their wrong choices over and over again.

Self - image is a contributor to wrong choice making. Humanity seems to have a real problem with this. We either think too highly of ourselves and become prideful or either we go to the other end of the spectrum and think too lowly of ourselves.

If you have grown up being told that you will never amount to anything or that you don't deserve any better or all you have been around is people that consistently make bad choices, then

53

you're a prime candidate to have a miserable life. Anger will become your God, you'll say things like I don't deserve this, if you hurt me I'll hurt you worse, I can't stand to see you happy, nobody loves me, I hate God because He is letting this happen to me! The truth is we cause most things to happen to us by the choices we make.

Many today are in a spiritual **abuse situation**. That is they have made wrong choices so much that they lack the will to do better. They become addicted to making mistakes. In their subconscious mind they become convinced that they can do nothing right.

<u>Wrong</u> <u>emotions</u> can contribute to our making wrong choices. Feeling inferior, depressed, embarrassment or fear of embarrassment hopelessness, loneliness, and disappointment, just to mention a few.

When all these emotions are at work in us it is hard to focus on what is right, we don't see clearly. In fact we most often don't see things as they are, <u>we see things as we are!</u>

ARE YOU WOUNDED?
IN LUKE 4:18

"THE SPIRIT OF THE LORD IS UPON ME, BECAUSE HE HATH ANOINTED ME TO PREACH THE GOSPEL TO THE POOR, HE HATH ANOINTED ME TO HEAL THE BROKEN HEARTED, TO PREACH DELIVERANCE TO THE CAPTIVES, AND RECOVERING OF SIGHT TO THE BLIND, TO SET AT LIBERTY THEM WHO ARE BRUISED.

54

CHOOSE TO BE FREE

Here Jesus declares the mission of the church to the world is to minister to them. Notice the latter part "to set at liberty them who are bruised." What is a bruise? It`s a spiritual wound of the soul. It is just like a flesh wound that bleeds. The spiritual wound only bleeds inside. Only the power of God can heal a spirit that is bruised.

If you are bruised you will not make right choices. So the first order of business is to get your spiritual wound healed. How? First of all, by acknowledging that you have one. Then, by repentance to God by forgiving who ever caused the wound, and by walking in the power of the word so that you can be healed!

When Christ raised Lazarus from the dead He did what no one else could do, yet after this He turned to His disciples and said "Loose him and let him go free."

Jesus will through His spirit and the word heal our bruised spirits if we allow Him to. Our part of the healing is to let go and free the past. We cannot bring any of the residue of our past life into our relationship with God without that relationship suffering greatly. Once you feel the joy of being free, you'll be able to make right choices based on your understanding Gods word. You'll also want to go loose some one else.

ARE YOU HEALED OR WHOLE?

Many today receive healing in their emotions, that is God does touch them and recover them from their guilt and shame. But because many times they do not continue in the presence of the Lord they are not made whole!

CHOOSE TO BE FREE

God makes it very clear in His word that He wants us healed and whole. What do I mean when I say whole? To be whole means not only am I healed but because I continue in fellowship with God, His spirit and word that is being applied to me daily has a tremendous impact upon me. The scars of sin are totally diminished, and my carnal mind no longer controls my actions and reactions. The Love of God is a constant in my life. I am truly walking in the spirit of the Lord. Now I am not only healed of my sin, but I am made whole, it has no affect on me. It`s as though I have been living for God all of my life. This is what God desires for us!

When you are made whole the word of God is alive in your spirit. You make choices based on what the word of God has to say about the issue. You seek His face to know His will about every action of importance. This helps you make right choices.

DEFEAT OR VICTORY
IT`S YOUR CHOICE

So what things dominate your life? Examine yourself and you will find this to be an index to your true self. You'll also find it is a key to your effectiveness or ineffectiveness.

Dominating influences and thought patterns work in two directions in our lives. They either defeat us or deliver us. **I am responsible for what dominates me!**

CHOOSE TO BE FREE

It`s entirely up to me whether I am controlled by wrong choices resulting in defeat, or by right choices which result in victory. It`s my choice! God built into every man the freedom to choose, it`s in the framework of mans nature. We can enlarge that freedom or forfeit it, depending on our choices!

So, always remember no matter how dark the day, choose to live on no matter how sad the circumstances. Most of all no matter how winding the journey to your freedom may seem, always go on!

We will all have pleasure and pain, sunshine and rain. We will all laugh ourselves to tears one day then cry ourselves to sleep the next. But remember, if we make **God - conscious** choices then what ever is wrong can be repaired. If you have lost your way don't give up, reach up to God. He is able to point us back in the right direction if we ask Him to.

PSALMS 23:3
"HE RESTORETH MY SOUL"

If your choices that are determining your decisions are not lineing up with your destiny, then listen carefully to the voice of God, He will speak in your soul and He will restore it from the pain of wrong choices.

PRAYER: In the Name of Jesus, I release the word to begin to heal my mind, my emotions, and my life. I repent of wrong, cleanse me daily through the power of your spirit. Help me to begin to walk in agreement with your word O God.

CHOOSE TO BE FREE

**SCRIPTURES TO RELEASE INTO YOUR LIFE THAT WILL HELP
YOU MAKE RIGHT CHOICES!**

ROMANS 5:8	JOSHUA 1:8
GENESIS 1:27	I CORINTHIANS 9:25,27
ROMANS 5:10	PSALMS 32:8
ROMANS 10:6-10	PROVERBS 1:1-22
ROMANS 8:31-39	GALATIANS 5:22-26

PROVERBS 3:5-6

Free From Bad Habits and Addictions

CHOOSE TO BE FREE

Let`s talk about bad habits and addictions. This is a problem with the human race. Even many in Christian circles have not yet been set free from some of these "bad habits" and "addictions." In fact many feel helpless in these areas, they manifest themselves in our behaviors or attitudes. Hebrews 12:1 states "wherefore seeing we also are compassed about with so great a cloud of witness, let us lay aside every weight and sin,

and let us run with patience the race that is set before us." Notice the progression for freedom. First we see it is our choice to lay aside these things. Why should I? The scripture says we should do this because of the great witness of the Gospel and impact that the New birth has on us. Simply put, we can because a way has been provided for us to do so. Recently when Michael Jordan came out of retirement again to play basketball, a reporter asked him why he was doing this. His reply was it`s not for the money, "He evidently has plenty already," nor for the recognition, then why? His answer was "**Because I can**, the day will come that I can't but right now I can."

My friend, if you need victory over some habit or addiction you need to jump up right now from where you are, get Gods word, open it in your hand and shout so you, the devil, and God can hear it. I am going to be free **BECAUSE I CAN**! That's right we can, because of what Christ has already done for us on the cross. You can be forgiven and you can be spirit filled, yes, you! The word beset in the passage implies a habitual behavior. The scriptures promise "no temptation has overtaken you except that which is common to man"

(I Cor. 10:13). Your temptation or sin is not unique, others face it as well. The latter part of that verse promises that God will provide a "way out." What are you looking for, an excuse to give in or the way out?

WHY ARE WE IN THIS BONDAGE

We believe the lie of Satan instead of the Word of God. Jesus said that Satan was a "liar" (John 8:44). Satan lies to us. He uses deception to convince many that they are not free! Satan was the first terrorist. He is still a terrorist. He wants to destroy you and all that you are. He will tell you you've tried before and can't get free, you can't help it, it`s just the way you are", or "no one understands my battle"! These are all deceptions. None of them are true. Yet millions fall into this dungeon of despair every day.

Because we believe Satan's lie, we cannot see that there is a way out! We try to change our desires, we search for answers, yet may still believe we are powerless to really be free. Many have surrendered their will to Satan rather than to God. When Satan controls our thoughts, he controls our lives. When he lies to us about our lives and we believe him, then we are in bondage!

HOW CAN WE BREAK EXTERNAL BONDAGE

If we are going to be free from habits and attitudes that are diametrically opposed to what God really wants for our lives, then there are several things we can do.

CHOOSE TO BE FREE

First of all, we must desire to be free. We might even need not only to pray, but fast as well. Matthew 17:14-18 gives the account of a deliverance of a young boy. In fact Jesus disciples had tried to deliver him yet were unsuccessful! Why? Jesus answers the question in verse 20. "Because of your unbelief: for verily I say unto you, if you have faith as a grain of mustard seed, ye shall say unto this mountain, remove hence to yonder place, and it shall remove. And nothing shall be impossible unto you. Verse 21 is what divides the victory folks from the bound folks, and the people of action from the daydreamers. "Howbeit this kind goeth not out but by prayer and fasting. Now if you won't pray, you surely wont fast!

What is Jesus teaching us here? Several truths. Here are some of them. First, real faith is never blind! No one in their right mind would walk out to the end of a diving board never looking below to see if there is water in the pool and merely jumping, hoping there will be water in it! Yet this is the way millions try to overcome habits in their lives.

Scripturally, when we say "I believe" we are actually saying "I know". How do I know, because I have chosen to believe the promise of God instead of the lie of Satan. When Jesus said, "If you have faith", He was saying, "If you know you can break this bondage, it will happen to you." Bible faith is believing what you know is so! So when you pray with understanding from the word and also fast to help bring your flesh under subjection then you are exercising your faith. You have a faith experience (what you say) that releases a faith expression (what you believe is going to happen) that produces a "faith event."

Let's stop here just a moment and look at the difference between doubt and unbelief. There is a radical difference between the two. One is a matter of intellect. You doubt because you don't understand. Everyone wrestles with doubt from time to time! The other, though, disguising itself as intellectual is basically a matter of the will.

Doubt is difficulty to understand. Unbelief is disobedience! We see this in scripture in the earthly ministry of Jesus.

One group, though they found it difficult to understand and accept the things they were seeing and hearing continued to follow Jesus with open hearts and minds. They could not explain what they were seeing and hearing, neither could they deny these things! They could not logically account for Jesus' action. Yet, in their faith they admitted to the facts and continued to follow Him faithfully. They doubted, but they did not reject Him!

The other group of folks cannot deny the facts, but they try to explain them away. They try to discredit Jesus. This is how unbelief works. Unbelief is a choice that is made in the will of a person to reject anything that interferes with the self-life, anything that injures his pride.

Unbelief argues against truth because it does not want to commit itself to truth. Unbelief is disobedience wearing a robe of false intellectualism. Unbelief hardens the heart of a person. So we need to understand this. We must believe to be set free!

CHOOSE TO BE FREE

STEPS TO BREAKING HABITS

First of all, renounce your control and turn control of your life over to God. This will bring a revelation of truth that with God in you, you can change! Secondly, acknowledge that you have been deceived. For many, this is very difficult. We have to acknowledge our own efforts to deceive ourselves. Psalms 51:6 "You desire truth on the inward parts and hidden part you will make me to know wisdom." Until we admit that we have been deceived we won't accept truth!

Many people have deceived themselves for so long that they have difficulty believing they are deceived! It has become a life style for them. They are in bondage. People that are living in deception will make comments like this about the word or the sermon they have just heard! "Well that certainly wasn't for me, I am O.K. in that area." They try to justify their actions by the actions of others. This will never bring freedom! Jesus said in John 8:32 "you shall know the truth, and the truth shall make you free."

When we are honest with God and ourselves, we allow God's truth to free us! So don't make excuses about the habits and addiction that hold you, let God loose in your life!

Now you must submit to God's authority. This involves not only trusting God but also trusting the chain of authority He has appointed in your life to provide leadership and growth! God has placed us all under authority (Romans 13:1-7). Each of these authorities has a sphere of influence in our lives.

CHOOSE TO BE FREE

Pray audibly, "I submit to God and His word and not this habit or this attitude.

Then you must take personal responsibility. The key to breaking habits and attitudes is to take full responsibility for your actions. You are responsible for the sin that has habitual control over your body (Romans 6:13).

Through the blood of Jesus, by the power of His name and the indwelling of His spirit you can break out and be really free and really delivered!

GALATIANS 5:1
"STAND FAST THEREFORE IN THE LIBERTY BY WHICH CHRIST HAS MADE US FREE, DO NOT BE ENTANGLED AGAIN WITH A YOKE OF BONDAGE."

RELEASE THESE SCRIPTURES IN YOUR SPIRIT

JAMES 1:21   ROMANS 12:2
II CORINTHIANS 3:17,18   HEBREWS 4:12
EPHESIANS 6:10-18   II CORINTHIANS 10:4,5
                I JOHN 4:17

Rebuilding Your World

CHOOSE TO BE FREE

Do you ever feel trapped by your circumstances? Do you wonder where God is and why He has not answered your prayers? You are not alone. I suppose we have all been there and no doubt will go there again in our journey. It`s in those times our mind is preoccupied with the question of "Where is God?"

Gideon asked, "if the Lord is with us, why then has all this happened to us" (Judges 6:13)? Elijah cried, "Take my life for I am no better than my fathers" (I Kings 19:4).

When David felt trapped in a snare, the Lord rescued him. "If it hadn't been for the Lord who was on my side.....they would have swallowed us alive" (Psalms 124:1,3). A snare is a trap, something, to delay us, or to stop us all together. David declared, "our soul has escaped as a bird from the snare of the fowls the snare is broken, and we have escaped" (verse 7).

God asked Abraham to offer his son Isaac, not that God actually wanted Isaac to die, but to see how the faith of Abraham would react. Abraham would either obey God or rationalize that God was asking too much. It was Abraham's choice! Abraham obeyed. He forced his emotional self to obey the convictions of his faith. Abraham knew that the best way out of a snare is to be **OBEDIENT** to God. Now that you have chosen to recover from your wrong choices it is imperative that you walk in **obedience** to God's word. There will be times as you and God are rebuilding your world that you will feel as though you have failed or that God isn't with you.

Yet faith reminds us that God is always faithful and true. His eyes are ever watching over us. If we must always understand everything God is doing to obey Him, then we will obey Him very little. To obey only what we understand is to merely agree with God. On the other hand obedience by faith leads us to understanding the ways of God and the wisdom of God. So make the choice. Put your hand of faith in the mighty hand of God. Roll up your sleeves and go to work. God is standing ready to help you rebuild your world, to fulfill your destiny, and to know His will for you. He is excited about what's about to take place in your life! He`s been waiting for this day!

BUILD OFF
OF YESTERDAY!

Now that you have made the choice to be victorious, you must learn the time sequence of your life. Don't live in yesterday, but build off of yesterday. What is yesterday? It`s the time span that has just passed, that twenty-four hour period has been laid to rest in the tomb of time, never to be resurrected again.

We all have experienced yesterdays. The Prophet Isaiah in his writing in chapter 52 verse 12 declares "you shall not go out in hast---for the Lord will go before you, and the God of Israel will be your rear guard." God is going to take care of the past. The Prophet declared the Lord will go before you. This is a great revelation! He brings us security for tomorrow. He sends out His forces to direct us. He will watch so that we don't experience the same failures again. God's hand reaches back into the past, settling all the claims against our conscience.

CHOOSE TO BE FREE

He gives us strength to build from our yesterday to walk into the present, because we are at a place called **NOW!**

We are in a building program. To rebuild our world we must get to **NOW.**

Where is it? It`s not a neighborhood, it can`t be found on a map. Neither money, nor education, nor influence can get you there. It`s a place in your life that all of God`s people seek! It`s that place where your soul starts to sing and rejoice because you know God is with you. NOW is that place that God has been calling us to from the beginning. Most of us spend years trying to get there. In this place called NOW you can and will reach your fullest potential. God`s greatest blessings are for us NOW!

When you get to this placed called NOW you will discover **TODAY!**

What is TODAY you may ask? TODAY is the beginning of the rest of your life. From TODAY you can go anywhere you want to go! TODAY is the springboard to your future.

God has placed within each of us the potential and opportunity for success. It takes just as much effort to live a bad life as it does a good life.

Yet, as you know millions of people lead aimless lives in prisons of their own making, fighting battles that have already been won, simply because they haven`t decided what to do with their lives.

It always cost more not to do God's will than it does to do it.

Life's heaviest burden is to have nothing to carry. The significance of any person is determined by the cause for which he lives and the price he is willing to pay. What we set our hearts on will determine how we spend our lives.

We do not need to take lightly the dreams and hopes God has for us. We need to cherish them, they are like children birthed to us.

"NO WIND BLOWS IN FAVOR OF A SHIP WITHOUT A DESTINATION"

God plants no yearning in us that He does not intend to satisfy. Every man's destiny is his life preserver! Where do you want to go from TODAY? Let God help you rebuild your world. Let him resurrect your dreams!

STEPS TO REBUILDING!

Everyone faces defeats, they drain our energy and they alter the course of life. Yet, when we choose to do God's will and live the life He desires for us, we not only can overcome, but we will overcome. It`s our choice!

Now that you have chosen to be free, you've got to start to rebuild. This is not an **event**. It is a **process**. To rebuild your dreams and to release the will of God in your life you must be able to distinguish fantasy from reality!

CHOOSE TO BE FREE

HOW???

Know where you are and where you would like to be. This is key, even though you are making right choices now there will still be some turbulent times! Be willing to share your struggles with those whom God has placed around you to help you.

Don't just try to live in some hyped-up attitude or merely some positive attitude mentally. But rather have true confidence in what God is doing in your life because you are walking in agreement with His word.

Evaluate where you are and remember you didn't get to where you are overnight. Don't have a **quick fix** mind set. God is at work in you because you have made a choice to submit your life to Him, rebuilding is a step by step process, it is daily!

We often abort the possibility of success by attempting to do too much too soon. If you are rebuilding dreams or especially relationships that have been damaged, you are going to have to have some patience. Don't immediately expect the painful damage done to others to immediately go away. They too, are going to have to make some right choices just as you have done.

Shattered dreams are redrawn one stroke at a time. It takes time and great courage to tackle this kind of rebuilding. You must methodically set about positioning yourself to accomplish God's purpose in your life day by day.

PATIENCE

Patience is an indispensable element in rebuilding your dreams.

CHOOSE TO BE FREE

To rebuild from being hurt and broken does take time. Just remember God will get us to where we need to be and it will be on time! His time, because He is never late.

Because of this you must become active in the body of Christ if you are not already. Just being in the mere presence of faithful people and the atmosphere of victory that prevails in the church will continue to affirm your faith in God that you have made the right choice.

DO GOD'S WILL

Rebuilding your world is more than just setting a goal, it`s doing the will of God daily. You have come through the nightmare of wrong choices and of bondage. So now let God plant new visions in the fertile soul of your spirit. Don't continue to see disappointment, pain, and fear, rather shout as Nehemiah and all his people did "Let us rise up and build."

When we obey God and allow God to lead us at His pace we will always be victorious. This allows God to draw other people to our side as well to help us accomplish the task.

OPPOSITION

Be ready for opposition on the road to rebuilding your world. Satan never just gives up, he is always trying to conquer us and divide us from God's presence. Just remember we have chosen to be victorious. We are walking in agreement with the word so we have power from above. It`s our choice!

Always remember you are not the only person who is in this building process, God is delivering people all over the planet.

CHOOSE TO BE FREE

Remember God wants you to grow and be victorious. God wants to take the very thing that Satan attacks to derail the plan of God for man and use it to defeat Satan. That is us, **MAN**. God is using man to defeat Satan, aren't you glad!

You are not insignificant. In God's sight everyone is someone. It is no accident that God has made us all different as far as our personalities and approach to doing things. Learn to use what talents you possess. In doing this, you will allow other talents to be developed. We were created for achievement. We have been given seeds of greatness. What is greatness? What is real achievement? It`s doing what God wants you to do and being what God wants you to be.

As born-again believers we are a new creation, not **rebuilt sinners**. Psalms 139:4 says that we are "wonderfully made." God has made us special for a purpose. Every person has a gift. You and I are never where we ought to be until we are doing what we ought to be doing. Your life makes a difference. Although we're all different, no person is insignificant in God's sight!

TAKE A MOMENT AND GO
AHEAD AND SHOUT GLORY!

Remember as you are rebuilding your world with God's help, all the important battles we will face will be waged within ourselves. Do not put water in your own boat, the storms of life will put in enough on its own. Don't dream up thousands of reasons, why you can't do what God has called you to do, that is to be victorious.

JOHN 4:4
"GREATER IS HE WHO IS IN US THAN WHO IS IN THE WORLD."

"Pray daily, release God's word into your life, build a life for God and others will come to your side to inquire of you how they too can choose to be free."

Choose Victory

DECISIONS DETERMINE
DESTINY

The Bible says that a double-minded man is unstable in all his ways (James 1:8). It is not necessarily the difference between people that's the difficulty, its the indifference.

God wants us to be the most decisive people on the face of the earth. Why did He give us His word and His spirit? So we could live decisive lives!!

How can the Lord guide a person if they have not made up their minds which way they want to go?

The average man does not know what to do with this life, yet he wants another one which will last forever.

The most unhappy people are those who can never make a decision. An indecisive person can never be said to belong to himself. Those who are indecisive are like someone looking in a dark room for a black cat that isn't even there and all the while refusing to turn on the light.

Satan is the only one who can use a neutral person. Making no decision is a decision. It takes no decision to be a failure. Our decisions will determine our destiny both spiritually and naturally. We need to meet all problems and opportunities of our lives with right decisions. We must allow the word of God to be our guide. A great deal of talent is lost for a want of little decision. It has been said that decision is a sharp knife, that cuts clean and straight. Indecision is a dull one that hacks and tears and leaves ragged edges behind.

Faith demands a decision before it can work. Every

accomplishment, great or small starts with a decision. We will have the wrong foundation and won't know what to do if we are always indecisive. The Bible tells us clearly, "if we will not believe, surely ye shall not be established" (Isaiah 7:9). If we remain indecisive, we will never grow. To move on from where we are, we must decide where we need to be. Make the decision today to allow God's word to influence and direct your lives. We must start being what God says we are! So choose victory!

WHAT IS VICTORY?

Is it an emotional feeling? Is it an attitude? Is it something I can only enjoy at church? What is victory?

It's amazing but many within the kingdom of God really have no true understanding of what real victory is. To many, victory is something that is short lived, it's something that is always just ahead of them!

What is the biblical concept of victory? The biblical concept of victory has to do with something that is already done. Thanks be unto Christ who giveth us the victory. You see, the death, the burial, and resurrection of Christ secured and set in motion our victory.

Victory is a **spiritual** **position** in my relationship with God. It really has nothing to do with what I feel. In fact, we can never run victory down so that we have it! We are not fighting for victory, we are fighting from victory. Victory is our spiritual base from which we go out each day. Biblically we already have the victory, in fact, we always have victory. Now the big question we must ask ourselves is "am I walking in the victory that God has already given?"

God honors His word when we release it in our lives. If you want to be free of something then go to the word and gather all the scriptures that relate to your situation.

Begin to release the word of God into your life. The word of God is like a seed, it has to be planted before it can produce. God's word is a spiritual weapon. In John 6:63 (Amplified version) we read, "It is the spirit who gives life, the flesh conveys no benefit whatever. The words that I have been speaking to you are spirit and life." Jesus here is telling us that His words operate in the spiritual realm and they bring life.

Our words are containers of power! They carry either creative or destructive power. Even in Genesis 1:1-4 we see a spiritual principle unfold at the very beginning. We see light overpowering darkness. Is there darkness in your life? Then your answer to get rid of the darkness is not talk about it all the time, nor to defend it, but to get some light into the dark areas. Pour in light and darkness has to flee. Begin to commit the word of God to memory. Read and study the word on a daily basis. Plant the seed of the word in your spirit, you'll be pleasantly surprised at what will begin to grow. Choose victory.

SO WHO'S IN CHARGE?

If we are going to walk in total victory and be what Christ commissioned us to be, that is light and salt, then we must understand spiritual warfare and spiritual authority. There must never be a day that we are not aware of who or what is in charge of our lives. God wants to partner with us to bring us abundant life.

HELLO ADAM

In Genesis 1:26-28 we read the account of the creation of Adam. Adam was created in the image of God and created without sin.

81

He was intended by God to have authority over all the other things God had created. God gave him authority and told him to have dominion and to subdue the earth. Man became the ruler under God and man was to be the physical carrier for the spirit of God in the earth. Adam was created with a free will (the ability to choose). God wanted his willing submission, not forced submission. So God gave him the ability to choose. Adam was to use all the resources of the earth in the service of God and man.

(Gen 2:15-17) "And the Lord God took the man and put him in the Garden of Eden to tend and guard and keep it. And the Lord God commanded the man, saying, you may freely eat of every tree of the garden: But of the tree of the knowledge of good and evil.....for in the day that you eat of it you shall surely die."

If Adam would give God his best, which was his free will, then God would give Adam His best, the best of everything. God was entering into a covenant agreement with this man. Of course we all know that Adam made a fatal choice that produced chaos. He took the authority God had given him and turned it over to Satan.

The Lord God had given Adam authority and freedom and everything that he would need to live a peaceful, powerful, and joy- filled life.

When Adam did what God instructed him not to do, by his own choice he became a captive of Satan who had enticed him into going against God's word.

CHOOSE TO BE FREE

LOOK AT THIS

In the New Testament, Luke records what Satan said to Jesus, while He was being tempted. (Luke 4:5,6) The devil said all dominion and authority over the earth has been turned over to me, and it is mine." How did he get it? Adam gave it to him. Adam had been given a lease to the earth by God, and he had turned it over to Satan by making a bad choice. This is why Paul instructs the Corinthian church (II Cor. 4:4) that Satan is the god of this world, or we might say the god of this world system. Whatever it is in your life that you have turned over to Satan, it is time to take it **BACK!**

HELLO GOD!

The good news is that God has a plan. In fact, God has never been without a plan of redemption for his man. The two Greek verbs translated redeem in the New Testament means "to buy" or "to buy out" to "release by paying a ransom price" (W.E. Vine commentary). God instituted His plan of redemption immediately upon discovering that Adam had disobeyed.

Genesis 3:15
"And I will put enmity between you and the woman, and between thy seed, and her seed, it shall bruise thy head, and thou shalt bruise his heel."

To bruise the head means to affect authority. God said that the woman's offspring (Jesus) who came by a woman in the fullness (at the right time) of time will take away Satan's authority.

CHOOSE TO BE FREE

When Jesus died on the cross for us He paid the price for our sins and for all sins. He also redeemed us and took back or bought back the authority from Satan that Adam had given him. He has returned it to those who believe and are born again and to those who also understand that Satan no longer has authority over the believer. This is what God has already done for us.

For years I believed that through the new birth of course, that I was born again and would go to heaven someday. Yet, I still struggled with this victory thing! Once I understood spiritual authority, how to walk in it, and how to locate the seat of spiritual authority in my life through God, then and only then did I realize there is a life of victory that God wants for you and me now!

Our position "in Christ" is one of being seated together with Christ in a heavenly sphere so that we may live by and through the authority that Christ has. **HALLELUJAH**

(Ephesians 2:6) "He raised us up together with Him and made us sit down together (giving joint seating with Him) in heavenly places (by virtue of who we now are) in Christ Jesus."

My friend it is impossible for us to live victoriously in earth without understanding and operating in our rightful authority and dominion over the devil and all his works.

God desires to restore you and me to the place of authority that is ours. He has already made all the arrangements. It is up to us however to choose Christ and obey His word that we can release and set in motion these wonderful promises.

(Ephesians 1:7) "In Him we have redemption (deliverance and salvation) through His blood, the remission (forgiveness) of our sins (shortcomings and trespasses), in accordance with the riches

84

of the generosity of His gracious favor."

RELEASING DIVINE POWER

Now that we know that we can choose to be victorious the next step is to understand how to release God's power into our daily lives. We do want to be free? Right? Let me pause just a moment to shock you again. We hear much today about <u>knowledge</u> being power! This my friend is only half true. The whole truth is this <u>knowledge that is</u> put <u>into</u> action is <u>power</u>! It is vital to our victory that first we have the proper knowledge of God's word but we must also put it in use in our lives then and only then does it produce power.

So are you getting excited yet? Here are the steps to releasing diving power into our lives.
(II Peter 1:3) "as His Divine power has given to us all things that pertain to life and godliness, through the knowledge of Him who has called us by glory and virtue."

God has already made this available for us. Why then is this not working for me you may ask? We either have not yet accepted God's gift and been born again, we did not understand the authority given to us through redemption, or either we are merely walking in disobedience to His word!

CHOOSE VICTORY NOW!

Step One - Be aware that "His divine power has given to us all things". Remember this statement made by Peter is not in the future tense. Peter declares God has already given us His divine power and through that power He has made everything <u>we need available.</u> When we begin to release this into our lives my friend, we will experience real victory. We will become the **"DEVIL'S WORST NIGHTMARE"** instead of it being the other way around.

Paul confirms this in (Philippians 4:13) "I can do all things through Christ who strengthens me." Again in (Colossians 2:9) Paul writes to the church "For in Him (Jesus) dwells all the fulness of the Godhead bodily; and you are complete in Him; who is the head of <u>all</u> <u>principality</u> and <u>power.</u>"

Read it slowly my friend, don't miss what Paul is saying. He is not only declaring that Jesus was God manifested in the flesh but he is declaring because of what Jesus accomplished on the cross and because of who He is (THE GOD MAN) that He has reestablished the seat of authority back to its rightful owner! **<u>Glory</u>**!!
If we have chosen to be a part of His kingdom then we are complete in Him! What does it mean to be complete in Him?

When you have Jesus Christ as Lord of your life, you have everything you need! We must remember that God <u>has</u> <u>given</u> us His divine power. (Acts 1:8) Peter is calling us to live by the power which comes to us through the <u>knowledge</u> of Jesus who has called us by glory and virtue. We walk and grow up in this by obeying His word.

LOOK!!

Now verse 4, "by which have been given to us exceedingly great and precious promises, that <u>by</u> <u>these</u> you may be partakers of the divine nature......."

CHOOSE TO BE FREE

The promises of God are great and precious! The word "precious" has the meaning of being "very valuable or costly. Why are they precious to us?

First of all because they allow us to be "partakers of the divine nature." This is exactly what happened to the disciples and those who gathered in the upper room at Pentecost. The spirit baptism imparted to them His divine nature to take the place of their own nature. The good news is this promise is still for us today and our children (Acts 2:39).

The implication of these promises are incredible for us. We have the potential to live by the very power of God. The second thing this precious promise provides is it allows us to escape "the corruption that is in the world through lust." Paul writes in (Galatians 5:16) "walk in the spirit (release authority of the spirit in your life) and you shall not fulfill the lust of the flesh." We must know which spiritual authority we are operating in daily! Peter continues with a list of things for us to add to our lives "give all diligence to our faith." What does he mean? Continue to build your faith and add knowledge and virtue. Faith is not blind. True faith doesn't exist in some hyped-up spiritual vacuum. True faith is released when knowledge of the word is released through obedience to the word. Stop worrying about what everyone else is trying to tell you to do to solve all your problems. Go to the source, God, and His word, and believe it above everything else.

Verse 6) Peter says to add self-control to our knowledge. This my friend is how you walk in victory. To know is vitally important, but it's not enough. We are to do what we know we should do. In many of our lives, there is a great gulf between our knowledge and our conduct! We need to be God-controlled.

Only when we are under His control can we have true self-control. The next step to releasing divine power in our lives is in verse 6, "add godliness". Godliness can not be fabricated.

We can not pretend to be godly. Why? The quality of godliness comes from God Himself who is living in us.

The more we are possessed of God, the more we will act like Him and the more His character will be revealed in our lives. Satan wants us to be useless and idle. God wants us to be fruitful. To release divine power within us we must live as Jesus instructed us in John 15:4 "Abide in me and I in you. As the branch can not bear fruit of itself, except it abide in the vine, no more can you except you abide in me."

We have too many people trying to live Christian lives on their own! This produces everything except what God desires for us.

WHY DO YOU CRY
TO ME?

God asked this question of Moses concerning the children of Israel while they were at the banks of the Red Sea. There are some valuable life lessons to be observed from this story. It unfolds in Exodus 14:10-20. Here we see in verse 10: the Egyptians coming after Moses and his people. The people begin to complain and be afraid. You see they still did not realize that the victory was already in place, it was not something they had to reach out after! Moses in verse 13 says "do not be afraid, stand still, and see the salvation of the Lord, which He will accomplish for you today."

What does Moses mean? First, he is trying to get the people to refocus on the will of God for their lives. We all need to refocus often. Then he says **stand still**. Stand still here implies the idea of a soldier who would stand his watch. Regardless of circumstances or what he may feel, he has been given territory to protect so he stands regardless of the weather or anything else Moses is saying don't let fear rule. Stand on the foundation of God's promise to us. God has already committed Himself to us if we will only go forward. This is real victory! We all fear what we have not yet experienced or where we have not yet been! Remember it is the will of God that we always go forward.

What happens when we do this? Well verse 14 gives us the answer. "The Lord will fight for you, and you shall hold your peace." The question here we must answer is am I going to fight or am I going to let the Lord fight for me?

When we understand that victory is part of our foundation of salvation and revelation then we will move forward This sets in motion the spirit of God to go before us! Remember victory has already been given! When we let God fight the battle and we stand in the authority of our victory then the peace of God that passes carnal understanding will be ours. It's called trust in God that He is really in control. God can do very little in our lives until we begin to move in the direction that He has already declared He would have us to go. Yet before there is any movement at all we must make a choice! No one else can do it for us. Look at verse 15, God asked the question of Moses, "why do you cry out to me'? Now this must have taken Moses back a bit. Yet there is a very important principle here we will miss if we are not careful. What is it? Here it is, God had already told Moses and the people to go forward. Yet, they are still here, still afraid, still waiting for God to do it all! God will not do anymore for us until we do what we know He wants us to do. His question is, "Why are you still asking me? I have already spoken to you about this. How many people do you know that will understand from the word what they need to do yet, they will just keep on and on praying to God about it for Him to do something!

Just like God told Moses don't talk to me about this matter any more, just go forward like I have instructed you to do. Are you there? Wondering why God hasn't moved in your situation? Why hasn't He answered your prayer. He is waiting for you to do what He has already commanded. You can't be having panic attacks and at the same time saying I have the peace of God. You have to know that God has made His peace available for you and then choose to move forward in that promise and it will happen.

Until we do what we know God would have us to do we will never get on the other side of our "Red Seas". If you are needing healing and yet are not living in obedience to God's word for your life the first thing you must do is to go forward in obedience then ask for healing. God is not going to do for us what He has already told us to do. You don't need to cry about, pray about, or complain about it. You just need to step forward in obedience then and only then can God work!

God says to Moses "Tell the children of Israel to go forward". God's question on the floor was this: What is it about go forward that you don't understand? "But God, there's a Sea in front of me, a mountain in front of me or whatever. Yet His command is still go forward!

Now look at verse 16, "But lift up your rod, and stretch out your hand over the sea and divide it." God is telling Moses I have given you the authority to lead these people to my promise for them. So, use that authority, speak in obedience in my name and it will happen. God knew the water would divide. Just as He knows you and I can be free from anything that tries to bind us and keep us from our victory in God. Yet it will not happen until we go forward in obedience and understand the spiritual authority that is given in Christ! This is why there are so many unhappy, dysfunctional "Christians", they are spiritually lazy, and non-committed. They want God to do everything for them! It simply doesn't work that way!

Are you wondering why God hasn't done something for you that you have asked Him to do? Could it be He is waiting for you to go forward! What's going to happen when I go forward? The Red Sea will either open up or you will walk on water! Because you have chosen to walk in victory! Now look at verses 19 and 20. The Angel of the Lord went before them and behind them. When they moved forward in obedience they also released the ministering spirits of the Lord to assist them in their victory. You and I do the same today my friend. It's time to understand our victory is already available. We must decide to move forward in it. Then God will arise and our enemies will be scattered!

"CHANGE IS NOT CHANGE UNTIL IT IS CHANGED."
"MOST PEOPLE JUDGE OTHERS BY THEIR ACTIONS, AND THEMSELVES BY THEIR INTENTIONS."

Intention to change is not change. Talking about change, pledging it, and making resolutions concerning it, will yield nothing until you decide you CHOOSE TO CHANGE!

RELEASE THE WORD

In Luke 6:5, Jesus asks the question of His disciples, "Why do you call me Lord, Lord, and do not what I say"?

91

Christ is looking for people who will do what He says. Obeying God's command is always the way to victory. Experts tells us that over ten thousand thoughts go through our minds each day. Let some of those include the more than seven thousand promises of God found in the Bible.

The Devil will fight you right here! When you choose to release the promise of God in your life. He will clutter your mind with wrong, doubt and false guilt. Take authority over him in Christ. Choose victory. Abraham believed God's promise and there was a promise land. Moses believed it and there was an exodus, a Red Sea dividing, and bitter waters made sweet, and manna and water from the rock. Joshua believed God's promises and there was a crash as Jericho's walls fell. David believed it and Goliath fell. The early church believed God's promises and there was an out-pouring of the Holy Spirit and miracles.

You might be reading this and saying this sounds good, in fact it sounds too good to be true. Is there a catch somewhere? The answer is yes, there is a catch. The promises of God are for those who have committed their lives to the Lord! They have made a choice to walk in victory. To obey His word!

USE YOUR KEYS

Matthew 16:19, "and I will give you the keys to the kingdom of heaven, and whatsoever you bind on earth will be bound in heaven, and what so ever you loose on earth will be loosed in heaven."

In this chapter of Matthew, Jesus asked His disciples the question "who do men say that I am? "(Verse 13). Then in verse 15, He nails it down, he confronts the disciples and says to them,

CHOOSE TO BE FREE

"But who do you say that I am?" There is spiritual authority that has been given to us that can never be released. Until we answer these question, it is imperative that we know who the Lord is. How then do we find out? By going to His word. In His word He reveals His nature, character, will, and all that He is. It's all in His word.

In verse 16, Peter under divine revelation declared Him to be "the Christ". Jesus responded to this and said, "Peter, flesh and blood has not revealed this to you". That is you didn't figure this out on your own. "But spiritual revelation has come to you Peter."

God wants us to have authority, yet to have it we must have some spiritual revelation, too. Now Jesus" response to Peter in verse 19, "I give you keys to the kingdom of heaven". What do you do with keys? You open doors right? Our problem however, is many times we don't know which key goes where, so it doesn't work for us. We must learn how to properly use the spiritual keys that have been given to us.

Part of being free is learning how to walk in step with God. At one point in this chapter, Peter has divine revelation. Yet in verse 23 of this chapter, Christ is telling why He has come to die for the sins of men. Notice verse 22, Peter takes the Lord aside and begins to rebuke the Lord. He says, "Far be it from you Lord; this shall not happen to you".

Peter is now thinking from a selfish carnal stand point. He is literally saying Lord I don't want to hear this. I won't let this happen, I'll get a sword! I'll protect you! Many times we are guilty of trying to protect our human pride or our preconceived ideas about something or someone more so than doing the will of God. This is why many are in bondage in their spirits today. The church is not here to hide in a corner or to merely condemn everything it doesn't understand. The church is here to declare war on the devil and his evil spirit of deception that is destroying and holding millions in captivity.

Many times instead of using the keys of revelation to release the will of God we try to lock up God's will and merely release our will!

Look with me at verse 23: Jesus turns to Peter and says, "Get behind Me, Satan". WOW!! Why would the Lord say this? Peter is now yielding to his carnal thinking instead of the word of God. Who influences our carnal thoughts? Satan!! That's why Jesus declared this "get behind me, Satan!" Poor Peter astonished and scared, no doubt, says, "but, but Jesus it's me your beloved trustworthy disciple Peter! Yet Jesus is teaching us here that we must operate in His authority and use the keys He has given us (His word) properly or else we will start thinking like Satan wants us to think. That always produces problems. Look at the rest of this, "you are an offense to me, for you are not mindful of the things of God, but the things of men."

When we walk and make our decision and our commitments based on our carnal reasoning we offend the spirit of God. We stop thinking with a renewed mind and start thinking with our carnal mind. Romans 12:2 "be transformed by the renewing of your mind, that you may prove what is that good and acceptable and perfect will of God".

Peter at this point had no real concept of what Jesus had given him because he was trying to impose his idea and his will on the Lord! I think we have all been guilty of this from time to time.

When we renew our minds, stand in spiritual authority and move forward then the keys will work and God will be glorified. So if you have tried and failed don't spend the rest of your life complaining or blaming God. Find out why the keys didn't

work and correct the problem. Choose to be free, it's a guarantee
that God has given us all!!

Who wants to Fight?!!

CHOOSE TO BE FREE

To be free we must know there is something from which we have to be free from! There is a warfare going on. Our war is not with people! Did you get that? **People are not our problem**!

The spirit that influences people is where the real problem is!

II Corinthians 10:3: "For though we walk in the flesh, we do not war according to the flesh."

Our battle is in the heavenly sphere and until we wage war there, we are not fighting at all. We are merely marching in a parade. In fact, that's what many do each week. They just march in and out singing to themselves, preaching to themselves, and going home just as bound, just as defeated and just as confused as they were when they came! They get mad at the preacher if he says the wrong thing, they'll get mad at someone for getting in their seat, or they'll get mad at a family member or each other. Yet, they will never get mad at the <u>evil one</u>. Satan loves this. He knows that these kind of folks will never take authority over him and get him in their sights. They think people are their problems. They don't even know where the real battle ground is!

To be free we have to take authority! All power and authority is given to us in Christ Jesus! It's not our authority, it's His authority which is released in us. God has given us six (6) pieces of armor to fight with. Three of which we are to never take off. The other three to pick up and use as needed (Ephesians 6:11,17).

The first three: (1) "The belt of truth." Truth needs to always influence your actions and decisions. (2) "Breastplate of righteousness." Know that if you're born again, the spirit of righteousness is at work in you. You are in right standing with God

(3) "Feet shod with the preparation of the Gospel of Peace." That is the peace of who God is and what God is doing in our lives daily to help us make right choices.

Then, the other three we need to keep close so we can pick them up at any moment. (1) Shield of Faith, (2) Helmet of Salvation, (3) Sword of the Spirit.

Here's how we access this authority, put it on and use the armor. Paul gives the key in Ephesian 6 after he had described all the armor, he then says in verse 18, "praying always, with all prayer and supplication in the spirit." Prayer is what opens the door to spiritual authority. When you pray you release and set in motion the authority of God in your life.

In a war, the first thing the government wants to establish is air supremacy Why? When you control the air then you'll have less casualties on the ground. Many in their spiritual walk have become a casualty because there was no "air power." (Prayer)! How does this work?

Remember, the church is to be going forward not running to hide. In the bible demons are on the run, not the Christian. Many today are merely on a spiritual treadmill, they are walking real fast but literally covering no ground.

In verse 14, we are told to stand. Stand on the territory that God has given you. Most folks have already lost too much territory. Territory of joy, of peace, of blessings, and the territory of a happy home.

What gives me this right? Again, you must understand that our war is in heavenly places. We are doing battle with fallen angels. To stand means you know your position of authority. Only when we understand this will we pray regardless of what is going on or not going on. You see, prayer is a withdrawal from our heavenly account not a deposit.

Christ has already deposited all we will ever need! Ephesians 1:3: "who has <u>blessed</u> us with <u>every</u> spiritual blessing in heavenly places in Christ". Through Christ's victory He established authority and rulership. When we are born again this is given to us. Everything we need is with Christ in the heavenlies. You say, "that sounds good, but I am here on earth". Read on, verse 17says, "the Father of glory may give unto you the spirit of wisdom and revelation in the knowledge of Him (Christ)". Verse 18: "the eyes of your understanding being enlightened that <u>you</u> <u>may</u> <u>know</u> what is the hope of <u>His</u> calling, what are the riches of the glory of <u>His</u> inheritance in the saints. His calling is to give us His authority working in our lives, His inheritance is eternal life through Him. Verse 19 declares: "the exceeding greatness of His power toward us who <u>believe</u>". If you don't believe, you surely won't pray. Look closer at verse 20: "hath seated Him at His right hand in heavenly places". Verse 21: "far above all <u>principality</u> and <u>power</u> and <u>might</u> and <u>domain</u> and every name that is named, not only in this age but also in that which is to come. Verse 22: "He put <u>all</u> things under His feet and gave Him to be the head over all things to the church". Verse 23: "which is His body, the fulness of Him who fills all in all"

These verses are telling us that the authority is already set in place. That everything I need He already has!

SHOUTING TIME!

Look now at Ephesians 2:6: "and raised us up together, and made us <u>sit</u> together in <u>heavenly</u> <u>places</u> in Christ Jesus".

CHOOSE TO BE FREE

This is it, we identify by knowing that what we need is in a heavenly place. Then we obey God's word and this puts us in right standing with Him. We understand He already has authority and that authority is released in our lives by the new birth. Paul continued because of the new birth and the understanding of who is in charge. We have been spiritually positioned with Christ. Where? In <u>heavenly places</u>. When we fight with this authority and direct the battle toward the real enemy we will always be victorious.

The reason people are bound is Satan is lying to them. They live in deception. In fact, Satan operates in a spirit of deception. That's all he's got. Jesus took everything else away from him! We must stop being deceived. We must choose our side with God. Then we must walk in authority, not mine, not yours, but in the authority of <u>Jesus Christ</u>!

So how is your <u>air attack</u> coming? When we realize what is already given, then all we have to do is release it. How? Through the avenue of prayer. Prayer is the <u>Christian's air supremacy</u>! Remember, in a war one army can have superior equipment, more soldiers, and more guns, and yet still lose the war if they do not know who their real enemy is, if they have no air supremacy, and if they are not sure what territory they are to secure! This is exactly what has happened and unfortunately is still happening to God's people.

It's time to claim our position. How do we do this? Through prayer. Prayer is our access code to the heavenlies. It's our opportunity to make a withdrawal from the heavenly account that Christ has already set us for! Only through prayer do we access the spiritual authority of God. Only through prayer do we really enter into the spiritual realm of the battle. We see in the Bible that when we pray, angels are dispatched. When Daniel prayed, Gabriel the Angel was dispatched. The scripture gives no indication of angelic activity until Daniel prayed! When you and I pray we set in motion spirits to assist us! WOW!! So why aren't you praying?

FIGHT FOR YOUR LIFE!

It seems that everyone is in some kind of battle. We have already discussed biblical ways to be free. Yet, there are millions who are still bound. They are **SPIRITUAL PRISONERS OF WAR!** Satan still has a hold on them through a spiritual stronghold that in many cases we have helped him to establish. It may be a stronghold of addiction, it may be a stronghold of the way your parents treated you and you may have never broken free from it. It may be a stronghold of a disappointment or a hurt that you have never gotten over! Some even have private strongholds, that is, strongholds of the mind.

A stronghold is a <u>mindset</u> that <u>accepts</u> <u>a</u> <u>situation</u> as <u>un-changeable</u> even though we know it's against the will of God. Strongholds are when Satan is operating in the spirit of deception in our lives. Satan has to use deception because that's the only tool he now has. Something is a stronghold when you are convinced in your mind that it is right. So, Satan uses deception to get people to willingly turn over their mind to the assumed idea that this is <u>just</u> <u>the</u> <u>way</u> <u>it</u> <u>has</u> <u>to</u> be! Are you captured? Don't blame others for your stronghold. You must address the stronghold from a spiritual standpoint. You can not fight a spiritual battle using things of the flesh. We fight against fallen angels not against flesh.

The first thing you must do to be free is you have to re-member your position in Christ. That is, you have to locate <u>your</u>

CHOOSE TO BE FREE

seat of spiritual authority in your life!
Ephesians 2:6 and Colossians 3:1

Once you are born again you are spiritually seated with Christ. Colossians 3:1 says to "seek the things that are above". You must always locate your spiritual seat of authority. Who or what am I going to allow to control me today? The choice is ours!

If your mind is set merely on a earthly solution then it is difficult to get a heavenly response! Your position in Christ, that is, declaring Christ to be you seat of authority (the one who rules) gives you power over Satan and his demented assaults against you. You can tell the angelic realm of fallen spirits that they no longer have any rights over your life.

When you are born again you have been legally set free and you have also been given authority over Satan. Satan does not want you to know this.

Christ, being the first fruit, regained man's rightful position. Colossians 3:15 says, "having disarmed principalities and powers, he made a public spectacle of them, triumphing over them in it".

The bible declares man to be made a little lower than the angels. So Satan, the fallen angel has authority over man until man becomes a new creation in Jesus Christ. Then, through Christ and the work He is doing in us, we now have authority over Satan. We are above him says the scripture. We win in Christ!! But to know this isn't sufficient, you have to walk in this authority. So locate your seat of authority, do it quick! Greater is He that is in you than he that is in the world!

CHOOSE TO BE FREE

WALK THE WALK!

James 4:6 declares that God gives grace. The real acid test to victory is to position yourselves in the spiritual authority Christ has made available. Yes, position yourself in Him so He can work in your life. James 4:7 declares, "therefore submit to God". Stop arguing with God. Quit trying to make it happen by your power. Submit to God! Walk in obedience to His word. The word submit means two things. It's important that we understand this. First, the word submit means to <u>SURRENDER</u>, then it also means to <u>COMMIT</u>! Many have this backwards. They come into the presence of God and then they commit to God while they are in a spiritual atmosphere. Yet, they go out never surrendering to God their lives, their wills, or their dreams. This is why people live in defeat. You must first surrender to God. That is, "God, You are in control, You are my seat of authority. I am walking now in a spiritual relationship with you daily, not giving in to my carnal reasoning". Once you have surrendered, you are saying God the battle is yours. I am going to let you fight, I am going to walk in victory. Then it becomes very easy to commit my ways unto the Lord. Not just a couple of hours Sunday, but everyday! This is spiritual power! What does the rest of verse 7 say? "Resist the devil and he will flee from you". My friend, until you locate your seat of spiritual authority, you will be confused about who to draw close to and who to resist! So don't just talk the talk, but walk the walk.

Fight for your spiritual life, fight for your family, do not surrender any territory to Satan. Fight for your church, your community, not by fleshly means but in the sphere of the heavenlies. Choose to be free. This war we are engaged in is unlike any other. This war has been fixed! That is, Christ has already secured the victory. God came to earth on Satan's own territory in the person of Jesus Christ and beat Satan in his own yard and took away the keys from Satan and He did it through the sacrifice of a body of flesh. God took the very thing Satan had tempted and weakened and used it to defeat Satan. God bruised Satan's head! In fact, Satan probably still has a headache! It's time we realize this and make sure Satan's head never stops hurting!

So, my friend, if you or I lose this war, it will not be because of Satan's attacks against us, neither will it be because God hasn't made all the provisions we will ever need available. The only way you can lose this war is you simply, by your own will and your own choice decide to just quit! The battle has already been fixed. We win!! All we have to do is access these truths in our lives that we have been talking about. So, get up and come on, let's walk together in the dimension of Apostolic authority that God has already given the church. Our time is short so we must move quickly. There is a world waiting for someone to show them how **TO BE FREE! MAKE THE CHOICE TODAY!!**